10 Ready-to-Go Math Performance Assessments

Teacher-tested, Reproducible Performance Assessment Tasks and Rubrics for the Math Kids Need to Know

Ruth Melendez

SCHOLASTIC
PROFESSIONAL BOOKS

NEW YORK • TORONTO • LONDON • AUCKLAND • SYDNEY
MEXICO CITY • NEW DELHI • HONG KONG

To my parents, Mary and Randall,
who taught me to dream.

To my best friend, mentor, and husband, David-
you always believed in me.

To my children, Julia and Christopher-
reach for your dreams,

and to the students I've had in math class-
thanks for taking a journey with me.

Cover design by Joni Holst
Cover photograph by Wendy Murray
Interior design by Joni Holst
Photos on page 62 and 77 by Wendy Murray. All other courtesy of the author.

ISBN 0-439-16515-6

TABLE OF CONTENTS

Introduction

How do you teach math? If you're anything like me, you teach math the same way you were taught in elementary school. Although I had switched to a process approach for teaching reading and writing several years ago, I continued to teach math as I always had done. My students sat at their desks completing worksheets while I worked with homogenous groups of students. I gave pretests and chapter tests, didn't use manipulatives, and taught a curriculum that emphasized computation. This was my mathematics program.

Each night I would sit at home in my oversize chair. Armed with my marking pen, I would carefully mark each problem with a *C* for correct or an *X* for incorrect. These papers would be sent home the following day. Looking back, I realize there was no spark, no joy, and no challenge in my mathematics classroom—for me or my students.

When we had to miss reading or writing, I would hear loud groans and variations of "I want to finish my story today!" But when math was canceled, I would hear lots of students cry out "yessss," and see them pull their right arms back as if they had just scored a winning run. I knew there had to be a better way.

SHIFTING GEARS

Once I recognized the need for a change, an alternative didn't immediately present itself. But gradually, as I talked to other teachers, attended conferences, and read professional literature, I began to experiment with new ways of teaching math. I introduced math centers to replace worksheets. I began to use manipulatives to teach concepts such as place value and regrouping. I encouraged students to reflect on their learning in math journals. The format of math class started to look like a workshop. We began each period discussing the problem of the day. Students worked in small groups to investigate this problem and then explained their findings in their math journals. Finally, we came together as a whole class to discuss the results of our investigation, comparing our thoughts and methods. Other days, students worked in math centers, where they practiced and applied skills related to our unit, while I worked with smaller groups or individual students. We did daily (but brief) computational practice. One day, I noticed students were enjoying math.

Yet, I continued to assess students in the same manner as before. And when I would sit at night with my marking pen, I would be disappointed because their scores on multiple-choice or fill-in-the-blank tests were not consistent with the work they were doing in their small groups or journals. And so my journey continued.

I needed another way to assess student learning. I wanted my assessment to reflect more of our daily problem-solving and writing activities. I wanted it to be purposeful and give students the opportunity to apply their knowledge and skills to a real-life situation. And I wanted students to have a clear picture of what quality work looks like.

ON THE ROAD TO PERFORMANCE ASSESSMENT

I found what I wanted in *performance assessments* and *rubrics*. A performance assessment presents students with a problem much like one that might happen in real life and asks them to use their knowledge and skills to solve the problem. The solution requires that students perform a task or produce a product. Each performance assessment is paired with a rubric that specifies what students must do to complete the assessment successfully. Students receive a copy of the rubric along with the performance task, so they can consult it at any time during the assessment and know from the start what is expected of them. There are no secrets about what excellence looks like when using performance assessments and rubrics.

WHAT YOU'LL FIND IN THIS BOOK

I've compiled ten of my favorite performance assessments with accompanying rubrics in this book. Each reproducible performance-assessment sheet lists the applicable math standards and benchmarks recently released by the National Council of Teachers of Mathematics (NCTM). I believe it's important that students know what skills we expect them to master and that they understand and are familiar with the language of the tests we give them to measure their skills. Also, putting the standards here allows parents to see what they are and how their children are working toward achieving them. Included on the sheet is an explanation of the authentic assessment task. The assessment sheet ends with the enabling skills that students need to complete each assessment.

The rubric that accompanies each task breaks down the task into four components. For each component, I describe exactly what I expect from a paper for it to be *Advanced*. I also outline what would make a paper *Proficient, Basic,* or *In Progress*. There are blank rubrics at the end of the book, so you can adapt or create rubrics to suit your own needs.

Finally, for each performance assessment, I include student work that you can share with your students to give them an example of how the task can be completed. Discussing the qualities of Advanced and Proficient papers before they begin gives students a clear picture of what they are striving for.

CRUISING ALONG

Now in my mathematics classroom, students have come to expect a performance assessment at the end of each unit. I provide a "teaser" at the beginning of each unit. For instance, during our first day of studying tessellations, I tell students that to conclude our study, they will design their own tessellation.

At the end of a unit, I give a multiple-choice, short response test supplied by our textbook company. This, along with the work done in a student's math journal and the performance assessment, establishes a body of work that demonstrates student learning. It also indicates which students need further assistance or experience with the concept studied. Reteaching and reinforcement occurs in math centers or during our daily computation practice.

Now when I reflect on my students' attitude toward math, I notice a distinct difference from those early days. Groans have been replaced with enthusiasm; students eagerly approach math class. I witness their daily moments of discovery and their triumphs as they solve meaningful problems. And now, when I sit in my oversize chair grading math papers, I am glad that my teaching led me to the use of performance assessments and rubrics in my mathematics classroom.

CHAPTER 1

Designing Effective Performance Assessments and Rubrics

For the past five years, I have used performance assessments and rubrics in my mathematics classroom. The first year students completed two such assessments. Now students complete a performance assessment at the end of each unit of study. My experience has shown me the immense value of this type of assessment, but for a performance assessment to be truly effective, it must be well designed and implemented. This chapter describes the power of performance assessments and rubrics and how you can create and use them so students can get the most out of them.

PERFORMANCE TASKS

Performance assessments provide a more genuine view of students' mathematical abilities than do standard tests. A performance assessment presents students with a real-life problem. To solve it, they must draw on their knowledge of mathematical concepts and apply specific math skills. The solution demonstrates the students' command of the skills and concepts being assessed.

For instance, I recently asked my students to determine the cost of the food we wanted for our class party. They had to estimate the amount of food needed, determine the total cost of the food, and finally, calculate how much each student needed to contribute toward the total cost. I then asked students to prepare a written recommendation that was the basis of my final approval. With this one assessment, I was able to evaluate their ability to estimate, add, divide, and explain their mathematical thinking in writing. Instead of isolating and assessing one skill at a time, I was asking students to address an authentic situation that required the application of numerous mathematical skills.

RUBRICS

Rubrics are an essential part of performance assessments. The word *rubric* comes from the Latin *rubrica*, which literally means "red chalk." Nine hundred years ago, red ink was used by priests to print prayer books. Over time, the word rubric has come to mean a set of criteria used to assess the quality of a project, skill, or behavior. The rubric specifies what quality work looks like.

With a rubric to guide them, students know what they must

do to achieve a certain level of work. In a classroom I visited recently, I asked a second-grade student how to get a good grade in math. He replied, "If you get the problem right, you get an A. If you don't get it right, you get an F." This was discouraging to hear. The focus on "right" and "wrong" answers neglects the process students use to arrive at those answers and doesn't take into account a student's thinking about a problem. Having a clear understanding of what the problem involves and what the teacher's expectations are empowers students to achieve. Rubrics become a student's roadmap to success.

GRADING WITH RUBRICS

The breadth and depth of information rubrics capture about students' performance must too often be reduced to a single letter grade for report card purposes. The process of converting a rubric score to a letter grade is simple. A student who consistently scores in the highest quality level would earn an A. One who consistently scores in the lowest quality level would receive a D. It is rare that a piece falls into the same quality level for each component of the task. You can assign point values to each component and determine an average. (See example at left.) You can even assign more points to certain components depending on your emphasis. For example, the computational work done during a performance assessment of addi-

NAME Elizabeth		DATE November 13, 2000	

RUBRIC SCORING GUIDE: Crack the Code

	Partially Proficient		Proficient	Advanced
	In Progress	**Basic**		
Place Value	◆ A student could not understand or write the number correctly.	◆ Poster shows shapes for at least 3 digits. ◆ A student could not write the number without help.	◆ Poster shows shapes for at least 5 digits correctly. ◆ A student might need a little help to write the number correctly.	◆ Poster shows shapes for 6 digits correctly. ◆ A student could understand and write the number correctly without any help.
Instructions	◆ The instructions have fewer than 4 math words. They are difficult for a student to understand and follow.	◆ Instructions include at least 4 math words. ◆ Instructions may be a little difficult to follow.	◆ Instructions include at least 5 math words. ◆ Instructions are easy to understand.	◆ Instructions include at least 6 math words. ◆ Instructions are easy for a student to understand and follow.
Conventions	◆ Numerous errors in spelling and capitalization make the instructions difficult to understand.	◆ Four or more words are misspelled. ◆ Three or more capital letters and periods are missing.	◆ Two to three words are misspelled. ◆ One to two capital letters and periods are missing.	◆ There are fewer than 2 errors in spelling, capitalization, or punctuation.
Neatness	◆ The instructions and/or the code are messy and almost impossible to read.	◆ Instructions and/or code are messy and difficult to read.	◆ The instructions and/or code are readable but it takes some effort.	◆ The instructions and/or code look like a published work of art— very easy to read.

To compute a numerical score for this rubric, I assigned point values to each quality level. For place value and instructions, I assigned the following points: Advanced=10, Proficient=8, Basic = 7, and In progress=6. I weighed the other categories less heavily since they don't address math skills. For conventions and neatness, Advanced=5, Proficient=4, Basic=3.5, and In progress=3. This rubric would score a 78%.

tion and subtraction might carry more weight than the conventions part of the written work.

ANCHOR PAPERS

While rubrics are helpful roadmaps for students, it is even more concrete for them to see examples of other students' work and hear how a teacher evaluated it with a rubric. Therefore, each performance assessment and rubric in this book includes student samples, which are known as *anchor papers*. You can use these until you develop your own supply of student samples.

When introducing an assessment, I use anchor papers extensively to help students understand exactly what quality work looks like for a particular task. I show an overhead transparency of the anchor papers and ask students to rate them using the rubric from the performance assessment. We discuss the scores as a class. The anchor paper not only serves as an example of what their assessment might look like, but it also provides a target for students to shoot for. It shows them excellent work and helps them understand why it is excellent. Students gain experience rating papers, and they get to see the difference between proficient and advanced work. Occasionally, lively discussions will take place between students who disagree about what quality level a particular paper should be placed in. This dialogue is welcome because it requires students to defend their thinking about quality mathematical work.

For instance, when presenting anchor papers about place value (see sample at right) the classroom conversation might sound something like this:

Teacher: Using your rubric, take a look at this anchor paper. Can you crack this code? (See rubric on page 21, anchor paper on page 23.)

Student: There are 2 hundred-thousands, 2 ten-thousands, 3 thousands, 3 hundreds, 2 tens, and 4 ones. So the number is 223,324.

Teacher: That's the answer that is given on the instructions. So what would you give this paper for Place Value?

Student: Since the rubric says "shows 6 shapes correctly" and I was able to solve the problem, I would give it an Advanced.

Teacher: Let's go through and identify the math words that this student used. What words do you see in the instructions?

Students: Ones, first, count, how many, ones, number, tens, hundreds, thousands, hundred thousands, and answer. That's a lot of math words!

Teacher: So which rating would this student earn on the rubric for math words?

Students: The Advanced column!

The conversation would continue for the remaining components of the task. When finished, the class would have a strong understanding of what an Advanced performance assessment looks like for "Crack the Code."

Most of these assessments take at least two math periods. On the first day, I introduce the activity and show one anchor paper. If a paper contains answers, I cover them with sticky notes. On the second day, we generate a list of math words and often look at another anchor paper. The list of math words hangs in the classroom until the assessment is complete. This practice focuses attention on strong math words and helps students with correct spelling.

THE ROLE OF SELF & PEER EVALUATION IN PERFORMANCE ASSESSMENTS

Using performance assessments and rubrics allows for both self assessment and peer review. These are powerful tools in my mathematics classroom. Because they take additional class time, I usually only use one kind of evaluation for each assessment.

SELF EVALUATION

Practicing self evaluation trains students to become better critics of their own work. It requires them to take responsibility for their thinking and for their final results. Although the process takes time, it is well worth it. Remarks such as *Am I done?* or *Is this right?* have no place in a mathematics classroom where performance assessments and rubrics are used. If a student does ask such a question, I respond with one of my own: *What do you think your rubric score will be, and will you be satisfied with that?* I easily put the responsibility for the work back where it belongs: with the student.

When using self assessment, I ask students to evaluate their work according to the rubric before they turn it in to me. They examine the criteria for each component of the assignment and put their initials in the rubric box that, in their mind, best describes their work. I often see students correcting their spelling, checking their calculations, or clarifying their thinking during this process. It is interesting for me to note how students rated their work when I evaluate the assessment.

PEER EVALUATION

Revising mathematical work based on peer feedback is not a common practice, but I believe it should be. Receiving peer feedback before preparing a final piece of writing has long been a part of our writers' workshop. During math performance assessments, I extend this practice to my math class. I introduce peer evaluation after I have presented several anchor papers that we score as a class using the rubric. The experience of rating papers as a group ensures that we are all clear about what quality work looks like.

Once students have completed a draft of their work, I make a copy of each student's paper (with the name covered) along with the assessment directions and rubric. I pass them out and ask students to rate the draft they receive using the rubric. Students eagerly employ highlighting pens during this process to point out computation or spelling errors, the number of math words used, or sentences that are confusing to the rater. They also indicate the category on the rubric they believe the assessment earns. I encourage them to make specific comments and suggestions so students have some direction when they revise. I then collect the papers and hand them back to the appropriate students.

When rated papers are returned, students have the opportunity to incorporate the additional feedback into their final work. I love this process—it's like watching 25 "teachers" at work in my class instead of just me.

How do students feel about the process of self evaluation or peer feedback? I've observed that initially they are a bit resistant, probably because we have never encouraged students to evaluate critically and revise their mathematical thinking. Once they see that this process results in a better product, however, they are likely to spend the time needed to improve their work.

WRITING YOUR OWN PERFORMANCE ASSESSMENTS AND RUBRICS

Once you've tried the performance assessments and rubrics in this book, you'll probably want to adapt them to the needs of your particular students or create new ones of your own. Here are some tips I've collected through my own experience of writing and using performance assessments and rubrics.

CREATING A PERFORMANCE-ASSESSMENT TASK

Plan your performance assessment at the beginning of your unit. Identify the skills you want students to know. Then list the corresponding NCTM standards and accompanying benchmarks on your performance-assessment form (see the blank form on page 94). Thinking up front about what you want students to know at the end helps you plan your daily instructional activities.

Now comes the fun part. Think about your subject matter and brainstorm scenarios that answer the question: *How do people really use this knowledge?* Spending ample time contemplating this question ensures that students are engaged in a real-life, purposeful task.

Take your favorite scenario and develop a *role, task,* or *situation.* List this as the performance assessment task on the performance assessment sheet. The work they complete must demonstrate that students have clearly met the standard or learned what has been taught. Following are examples of a role, task, and situation taken from assessments in this book:

ROLE: You have been hired to create a tessellation design for the Maze Art Company. ("A-Maze-ing Tessellations," page 79)

TASK: Develop and conduct a survey about students' favorite desserts and then construct a graph describing your results. ("Lunch Time," page 88)

SITUATION: Today is your first day as the Honorable Judge of the Kids' Court. This is a very important position because you will be making decisions that affect kids. Here is your first case.... ("You Be the Judge," page 72)

Finally, list the enabling skills that students must know in order to complete the performance assessment. Listing these skills serves several purposes. First, it becomes a sort of checklist for you, helping you keep in mind the specific skills students need to know. In addition, it signals to students the skills they need to apply to develop their solution successfully. It also gives them the chance to approach you beforehand if they have problems in a particular area. Finally, it's a great way to communicate with parents about what is being taught in your classroom and how it relates to the standards.

WRITING THE ACCOMPANYING RUBRIC

Once you've outlined your performance task, it's time to create the rubric. First, decide on what you will call your quality levels. These are listed horizontally at the top. I use *Advanced*, *Proficient*, *Partially Proficient*, *Basic* and *In Progress*, because these are the descriptors that our State Assessment Program uses.

Second, break out the key skills, products, or behaviors the task is trying to measure. List them in the boxes down the left-hand side. For instance on the "Lunch Time" rubric (page 89), the skill is the data collection, the product is the graph, and the behavior is the group presentation. All performance assessments should list at least one skill since this is the academic component of the assessment. The product is what students produce during the assessment, and the behavior can include how many times a students needs guidance from the teacher, how well a group works together, and the amount of student effort or participation.

Once you've identified the components of the assignment, write short statements describing the criteria for the quality levels of each skill, product, or behavior. The tricky part here is making sure there is an easily identified difference between the quality levels. For instance, the difference between Advanced and Proficient in the tessellation portion of "A-Maze-ing Tessellations," (page 80) is that Advanced used at least two shapes that tessellate, while Proficient used just one shape. I find it easier to begin at my highest level and ask, *What would the highest quality of work look like?* Then I work to the left.

I have found that the most effective rubrics that I have developed have been in collaboration with my students. I don't always ask students to participate in this process because of time constraints. However, it truly engages students in the process of defining and producing quality work.

One final word about rubrics: They are a constant work in progress. As you begin to use rubrics to rate performance, you will see where changes need to be made to meet the needs of your students. For instance, you might have a class of students who have difficulty expressing their thinking in writing. So the writing component of the assessment might be revised to include specific expectations. Or, if labeling answers is a problem, this might be added to the expectations. The attitude that rubrics are a work in progress is important.

Place Value

t is essential that students develop a sense of number and place value. Without it, they'll have a difficult time performing basic mathematical tasks, such as estimating; adding, subtracting, multiplying, or dividing whole numbers; or completing mental math operations. You are probably fully aware of those students who lack a strong sense of number and thus struggle to explain the value of the digit 3 in the number 13,765 as compared with its value in the number 317.

I designed "Crack the Code" to assess my students' ability to compose and decompose a large number, a task that requires a firm grasp of place value. I devised the scenario of a frustrated teacher having difficulty teaching the concept of ones, tens, hundreds, thousands, ten thousands, and hundred thousands. I asked students to help out this teacher by creating numbers with codes. Then they had to explain to the teacher's students how to solve the code to determine the number. I wanted to be sure that, if students invented the number 123,678, they would understand that the 1 is worth one hundred thousand, and would be able to explain that concept clearly.

IN ADVANCE

I found it helpful to introduce this assessment as a whole-group game. I created a code, wrote it on an overhead transparency, and asked students to solve it using the key. They were intrigued with this sort of puzzle and wanted to create puzzles for one another to solve. At this point, I formally introduced the performance assessment. They were ready to go.

DURING THE ASSESSMENT

After students had created a code and written directions to solve it, I encouraged them to trade papers to see if they could crack one another's codes. Peers provided valuable feedback concerning the codes and directions.

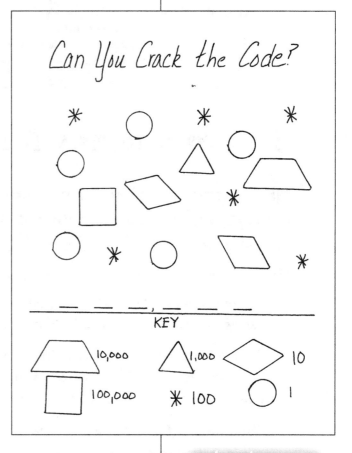

This is the sample code I introduce as a game. The answer is 111,625.

NAME   DATE

Crack the Code

NCTM STANDARDS	◆ Understand numbers, ways of representing numbers, relationships among numbers, and number systems. ◆ Solve problems that arise in mathematics and in other contexts.	◆ Organize and consolidate mathematical thinking through communication. ◆ Create and use representations to organize, record, and communicate mathematical ideas.
BENCHMARKS	◆ Understand the place-value structure of the base-ten number system and be able to represent and compare whole numbers.	◆ Recognize equivalent representations for the same number and generate them to decomposing and composing numbers.

Performance Assessment Task

Mrs. Frazzle is pulling her hair out! Her math students are having difficulty understanding hundred thousands, ten thousands, hundreds, tens and ones. She is asking for your help. This is what she would like you to do:

♦ **Design a poster that uses shapes to represent ones, tens, hundreds, thousands, ten thousands, and hundred thousands.**

♦ **At the bottom of the poster include a key that tells which shape goes with which place (for example, squares = ones; triangles = tens, rectangles = hundreds; and so on).**

♦ **On a piece of notebook paper, write a set of instructions that a student could follow to determine your six-digit number. Make sure you use as many math words as possible in your instructions.**

Enabling Skills	◆ Understanding ones, tens, hundreds, thousands, ten thousands, and hundred thousands ◆ Decomposing a number ◆ Writing clear and specific directions to determine the number

10 Ready-to-Go Math Performance Assessments by Ruth Melendez Scholastic Professional Books

NAME _____

DATE _____

RUBRIC SCORING GUIDE: Crack the Code

	In Progress	Basic	Proficient	Advanced
	Partially Proficient		**Proficient**	**Advanced**
Place Value	◆ A student could not understand or write the number correctly.	◆ Poster shows shapes for at least 3 digits. ◆ A student could not write the number without help.	◆ Poster shows shapes for at least 5 digits correctly. ◆ A student might need a little help to write the number correctly.	◆ Poster shows shapes for 6 digits correctly. ◆ A student could understand and write the number correctly without any help.
Instructions	◆ The instructions have fewer than 4 math words. They are difficult for a student to understand and follow.	◆ Instructions include at least 4 math words. ◆ Instructions may be a little difficult to follow.	◆ Instructions include at least 5 math words. ◆ Instructions are easy to understand.	◆ Instructions include at least 6 math words. ◆ Instructions are easy for a student to understand and follow.
Conventions	◆ Numerous errors in spelling and capitalization make the instructions difficult to understand.	◆ Four or more words are misspelled. ◆ Three or more capital letters and periods are missing.	◆ Two to three words are misspelled. ◆ One to two capital letters and periods are missing.	◆ There are fewer than 2 errors in spelling, capitalization, or punctuation.
Neatness	◆ The instructions and/or the code are messy and almost impossible to read.	◆ The instructions and/or code are messy and difficult to read.	◆ The instructions and/or code are readable but it takes some effort.	◆ The instructions and/or code look like a published work of art—very easy to read.

CRACK THE CODE

♦ **Advanced Paper**

Tasha's activity demonstrates an understanding of place value. She drew and then identified a six-digit number. Her directions are clearly written and use at least six appropriate math words (they are underlined in the sample). Her conventions are strong and her explanation is easy to read.

♦

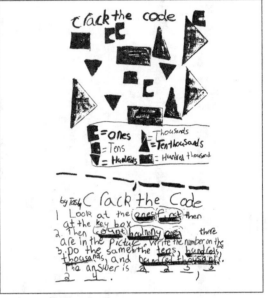

▲ **Advanced Performance Assessment for Crack the Code**

♦ **Proficient Paper**

Elizabeth's code indicates that she has the basic knowledge of place value, but her code does not match her answer, and her key is difficult to read. In the thousands place, she made six asterisks (*), but her answer indicates zero thousands. Also, she miscounted the number of hundreds. Thus, she was able to show four shapes correctly, but a student would need some assistance to write her number correctly. Her instructions were not as complete as Tasha's: they don't refer to the key box or to writing the number in the blanks. She misspelled some words, left out a capital letter, and had some areas that were a bit messy and difficult to read, particularly in the key box.

▲ **Proficient Performance Assessment for Crack the Code**

Crack the code

= ones
= Tens
= Hundreds

= Thousands
= Ten thousands
= Hundred thousand

Crack the Code

1 Look at the ones first then at the key box

2. Then count how many ones there are in the picture. Write the number on the line

3. Do the same for the tens, hundreds, thousands, and hundred thousands. The answer is 2 2 3 3 2 4 .

by Tasha

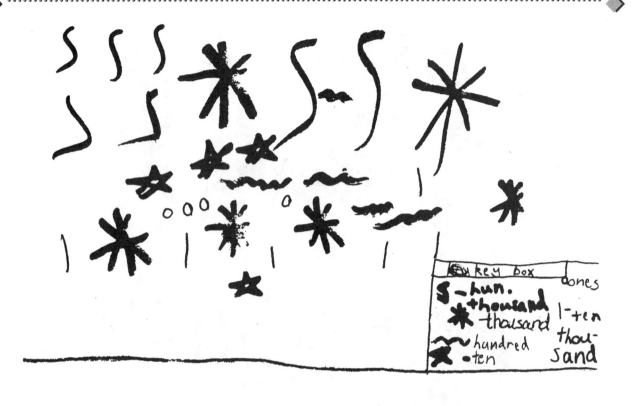

First you look at the <u>hundred thousands</u> then you <u>count</u> them. Then you do the same with the <u>thousands</u>. Next do the same with the <u>hundreds</u>. After that you do the same with the <u>tens</u>. last you do the same thing with the <u>one</u>

My answer is 760,644.

by Elizabeth

Addition and Subtraction

Addition and subtraction are basic math skills that students must master. This section focuses on adding and subtracting several digits, including zero. Giving students meaningful problems to solve fosters the development of computational skills while developing effective problem-solving strategies. (Worksheets that contain rows of practice problems do not.) Encouraging students to write about and discuss their thinking helps them build on their own understanding so they can apply it in real-life situations. As you read their journals and listen to their conversations, you'll be able to assess each student's grasp of these essential skills.

ADDITION AND SUBTRACTION PERFORMANCE ASSESSMENTS

The two performance assessments included here give students the opportunity to solve meaningful problems. The writing component helps students solidify their thinking and demonstrate to others what they know. "Toy Drive" simulates selecting and purchasing gifts for the local toy drive. I've used this assessment during the holiday season, when students' interest in perusing catalogs is at its peak. Students are motivated to complete this task and eagerly apply their math skills to the problem. They must also explain their choices by writing a letter to the toy-drive coordinator.

Reading aloud *Pigs Will Be Pigs* by Amy Axelrod sets the stage for the students to be financial advisers to this zany family of pigs. One of the challenges of the "Pig Family Finances" assessment is to organize the money scattered throughout the Pig family household. I use this opportunity to discuss with students how graphic organizers can help them record and use information. In this case, a graphic organizer can help them tally the number of different coins and compute the total amount of money in the house. Both assessments are designed to determine students' understanding of estimation, their skill in adding and subtracting with regrouping, and their ability to communicate their thinking in writing.

Both rubrics contain a section on neatness. I include this section on these particular assessments because, early on, I want to draw attention to the overall presentation of student work. This section can be added to any rubric in this book, particularly if you are concerned about the neatness of students' work.

NAME _____   DATE _____

Toy Drive

NCTM STANDARDS	◆ Compute fluently and make reasonable estimates. ◆ Solve problems that arise in mathematics and in other contexts. ◆ Apply and adapt a variety of appropriate strategies to solve problems.	◆ Organize and consolidate mathematical thinking through communication. ◆ Communicate mathematical thinking coherently and clearly to peers, teachers, and others.
BENCHMARKS	◆ Develop fluency in addition and subtraction. ◆ Develop and use strategies to esti-	mate the results of whole-number computations and judge the reasonableness of such results.

Performance Assessment Task

Your teacher has selected you to purchase $300.00 worth of toys to give to the local toy drive. You may purchase any items you wish as long as the total does not exceed $300.00. Here is your task:

- ◆ **Looking at the catalogs and advertisements provided, select the items you wish to purchase.**

- ◆ **On a piece of paper, list the items along with their prices.**

- ◆ **On the same piece of paper, estimate to the nearest ten the total amount you will be spending. Remember, it must not be more than $300.00!**

- ◆ **Calculate the exact price.**

- ◆ **On the same sheet of paper, calculate how much change you will get back from $300.00.**

- ◆ **On a separate piece of paper, write a letter to the coordinator of the toy drive explaining why you chose to purchase what you did and why you think the items will make good gifts.**

Enabling Skills	◆ estimating sums ◆ adding with regrouping	◆ subtracting with regrouping ◆ writing an effective letter

10 Ready-to-Go Math Performance Assessments by Ruth Melendez Scholastic Professional Books

10 Ready-to-Go Math Performance Assessments by Ruth Melendez   Scholastic Professional Books

NAME _____

DATE _____

RUBRIC SCORING GUIDE: Toy Drive

	Partially Proficient		Proficient	Advanced
	In Progress	**Basic**		
Place Value	• Work is not shown. • Many addition or subtraction errors. • Regrouping is not understood.	• Not all work is shown. • Several addition or subtraction errors. • Mistakes noted in regrouping.	• Work is shown. • Work has a few minor addition or subtraction errors. • Regrouping is correct.	• All work is shown. • Addition and subtraction work is correct. • Regrouping is correct.
Instructions	• Estimating is not attempted.	• Estimating is not shown. • Estimates are way off or answer is not correct.	• Estimating is shown. • Estimates may be a little off.	• Estimating is shown. • Estimates are reasonable. • Answer given is the correct estimate.
Conventions	• Letter format isn't followed. • Numerous errors in spelling, capitalization and punctuation.	• Letter format isn't followed. • Several errors in spelling, capitalization, and punctuation; however, it is readable. • No reason is given for buying the products.	• Letter format is followed. • Few errors in conventions; however, they don't take away from the letter. • Letter gives a good reason for buying the products.	• Letter format is followed. • One would have to look carefully for any convention errors. • Letter is creative and a pleasure to read.
Neatness	• No genuine effort put forth to produce neat work. • Reader has difficulty finding the information.	• Can see effort but reader cannot see different parts of task.	• Math calculations and letter move reader through entire piece.	• Math calculations and letter move reader through entire piece and there are no errors.

TOY DRIVE

◆ **Advanced**

Julia scored in the Advanced column in all areas except for the letter. All her addition and subtraction work is correct, including her estimates. Her work is well organized, neat, and it is easy to follow her thought process. Note that she initially had 11 items selected to purchase, but crossed out 2 of them so as not to exceed the $300 limit. Her letter contains several spelling errors, especially words that I would expect a third grader to spell correctly (i.e., *because* and *dollars*).

▲ **Advanced Performance Assessment for Toy Drive**

◆ **Proficient**

Gillian's work scored mostly in the Proficient column. Her addition work has one error; however, the regrouping is correct. Her subtraction work indicates that she needs more assistance or practice with the concept of regrouping with multiple zeros. Her estimating is nearly correct, except she rounded $149.94 to $100 instead of $150. Her letter and overall neatness are in the Advanced range, since her work is well organized and flows smoothly, and one would have to look carefully for mistakes in spelling, capitalization, or punctuation.

▲ **Proficient Performance Assessment for Toy Drive**

Julia

tocket $7.98

bean bag $52.50

glow poster $11.98

Stocking $ 12.98

sleeping bag $79.98

teddy bear $17.98

beany babby $9.98

cloths $30.00

snowman set $21.98

chess $59.98

art set $9.98

9 1
7 7.98   2 8.00
52.50   53.00
19.98   20.00
12.98   13.00
79.98   80.00
17.98   18.00
9.98   10.00
30.00   30.00
21.98   22.00
59.98   60.00
+ 9.98   10.00
_____   _____
$323.32 $324.00
- 25.96   - 26.00
_____   _____
$297.36 $298.00

2 9 9 9
$300.00
- 297.36
_____
$002.64

Dear Mary,

I chose all thease prodes becos I made an age groop 8-12 and I think Someone 8-12 would like the toys and stuff. I would! I think they would like a poster to put on the wall. A sleeping bag to snugle with and an art set to draw with. I got them a lot more stuff. It is a big list!

Sincerely, Julia

P.s. There are 9 toys and stuff all together and I spent #297 dollers and 36 cents.

56.5
59.99
14.99
19.99
19.99
14.99
19.99
#149.94

1 3 3 3
149.94
+ 24.99
39.99
79.99
294.92

1
60.00   100.00
15.00   25.00
20.00   40.00
20.00   80.00
15.00   245.00
20.00
#150.00

2
$00.00
− 294.92
#16.08

Gillian

Gillian
12-2-99

I made up a four year old and
that lives in an apartment that
doesn't have many toys. I bought
for her a wagon for 59.99, a

keyboard for 19.99, a video chair
for 19.99, a Betty spaghetty
for 14.99,
Art Activity set for 19.99 and a
furby for 24.99,
a laptop for 39.99,
and a Sonny the seal game for
14.99. I also got a bike for
when she gets older for 79.99.
I got all this stuff because When
I was a little kid I liked
that kind-of stuff and I thought
that she would like this kind-of
stuff too. My total added up to
$259.59. I have $59.99 until $300.00.

Sincerelly,
Gillian

NAME   DATE

Pig Family Finances

NCTM STANDARDS	◆ Compute fluently and make reasonable estimates. ◆ Solve problems that arise in mathematics and in other contexts. ◆ Apply and adapt a variety of appropriate strategies to solve problems. ◆ Organize and consolidate mathematical thinking through communication.	◆ Communicate mathematical thinking coherently and clearly to peers, teachers, and others. ◆ Create and use representations to organize, record, and communicate mathematical ideas. ◆ Select, apply, and translate among mathematical representations to solve problems.
BENCHMARKS	◆ Develop fluency in adding and subtracting. ◆ Develop and use strategies to esti-	mate the results of whole number computations and judge the reasonableness of such results.

Performance Assessment Task

Read the book *Pigs Will Be Pigs* by Amy Axelrod. The Pig family has hired you to straighten out their money problems. Complete the following steps to help them out:

◆ **Determine the total amount of money that the Pig family can find in their house. Please show your work!**

◆ **Estimate to the nearest ten cents how much money four specials would cost the Pig family. Please show your work! I wonder if they'll have enough money?**

◆ **Figure out the exact change the Pig family should receive from the waitress after they give her all their money. Show your work!**

◆ **The Pig family is having difficulty determining their total bill and change. Explain in writing how you solved one of your addition or subtraction with regrouping problems. Perhaps this explanation will help them the next time they go to a restaurant. Details do count!**

Enabling Skills	◆ estimating sums ◆ adding with regrouping ◆ subtracting with regrouping ◆ explaining how to add or subtract with regrouping in writing

10 Ready-to-Go Math Performance Assessments   by Ruth Melendez   Scholastic Professional Books

NAME _____

DATE _____

RUBRIC SCORING GUIDE: Pig Family Finances

	In Progress	Basic	Proficient	Advanced
	Partially Proficient			
Place Value	◆ Work is not shown. ◆ Many addition or subtraction errors. ◆ Regrouping is not understood.	◆ Not all work is shown. ◆ There are several addition or subtraction errors. ◆ Mistakes noted in regrouping.	◆ Work is shown. ◆ Work has a few minor addition or subtraction errors. ◆ Regrouping is correct.	◆ All work is shown. ◆ Addition and subtraction work is correct. ◆ Regrouping is correct.
Instructions	◆ Estimating is not attempted.	◆ Estimating is not shown. ◆ Estimates seem to be way off, or the answer is not correct.	◆ Estimating is shown. ◆ Estimates may be a little off.	◆ Estimating is shown. ◆ Estimates are reasonable. ◆ Answer given matches the estimate.
Conventions	◆ Explanation doesn't help the Pig family. ◆ No math words used. ◆ Many words are misspelled and end punctuation is missing.	◆ The Pig family would have at least 2 questions about explanation. ◆ The explanation uses at least 2 math words. ◆ Several words are misspelled or missing important end punctuation.	◆ The Pig family might have 1 question. ◆ The explanation uses at least 3 math words. ◆ Few minor spelling errors or missing punctuation marks.	◆ Detailed explanation uses at least 4 math words. ◆ Words are correctly spelled, and punctuation is correct.
Neatness	◆ Reader has difficulty reading and finding the information.	◆ Writer put forth effort, but reader has difficulty seeing parts of the task.	◆ Generally easy to follow the graphic organizer, math calculations, and explanation. Reader can make it through the piece.	◆ Graphic organizer, math calculations, and explanation help reader flow through the piece. ◆ Easy to follow.

PIG FAMILY FINANCES

◆ **Advanced Paper**

Shane's work fell within the Advanced range. His addition and subtraction are flawless, his estimates are reasonable and correct, and his explanation is detailed with at least four math words. His overall neatness also was scored at the Advanced range. His graphic organizer is easy to follow; the problems flow from one to another and are labeled, so it's easy to follow his

◆ thought process.

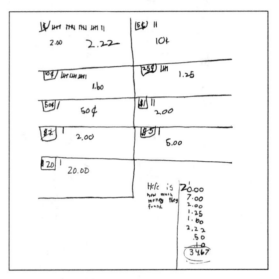

▲ **Advanced Performance Assessment for Pig Family Finances**

◆ **Proficient Paper**

Because Abby was having difficulty lining up her columns correctly, she used graph paper. Although her regrouping is correct, she does have some computational errors in computing the total amount of money the Pig family has, as well as the total restaurant bill; therefore, she scored in the Proficient range for addition and subtraction work. Her estimating is reasonable and correct, thus placing her in the Advanced range. Her explanation falls short because, while it contains words of encouragement for the waitress, it fails to use any math words and it doesn't explain how to solve the problem. In terms of overall neatness, Abby scored in the Advanced range. Abby chose to use the graph paper to assist her in organizing her numbers, and the problems and written explanation follow in sequential

◆ order. Abby's written explanation is a

▲ **Proficient Performance Assessment for Pig Family Finances**

good one to demonstrate the importance of communicating about one's thinking, rather than just giving an opinion.

1¢ ~~/~~ ◇◇ ◇◇ ◇◇ ◇◇ II

2.00   2.22

5¢ II

10¢

10¢ ◇◇ ◇◇ ◇◇ I

1.60

25¢ ◇◇   1.25

50¢ /

50¢

$1 II

2.00

$2 I

2.00

$5 I

5.00

$20 I

20.00

Here is how much money they found

20.00
7.00
2.00
1.25
1.60
2.22
.50
.10
34.67

Shane

This is my
estamation of how
much money it
will cost.

Shane

8.00
8.00
8.00
8.00

32.00

This is
the change
they will get
back.

3 3
7.99
7.99
7.99
7.99

31.96

3 16
34.67
− 31.96

2.71

4

On number three I did
34.67 − 31.96. I did 7−6=1
6-9 I can't do so I borrowed from
the one dollar billes and then crossed
the four out and made it a
three then crossed the six
out so it is 16. Then
I subtracted −9 then −3 and
my ancer is 2.71 ¢.

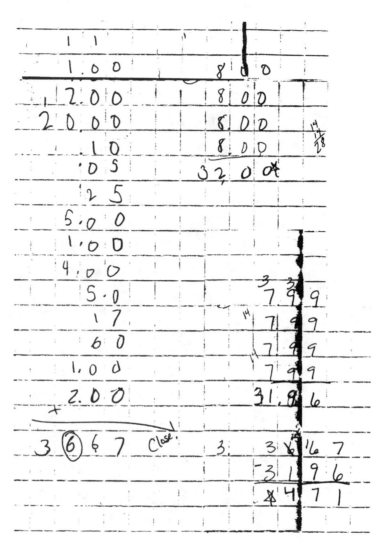

Abby

Well 7.99 is one
7.99
7.99
+7.99
31.96 ¢

it is easy if you
concentrate. if you you
try it it is easy mrs.
chicken. try it. It was
hard for me too. some times
you can you use duta and
math words.

CHAPTER 4

Multiplication

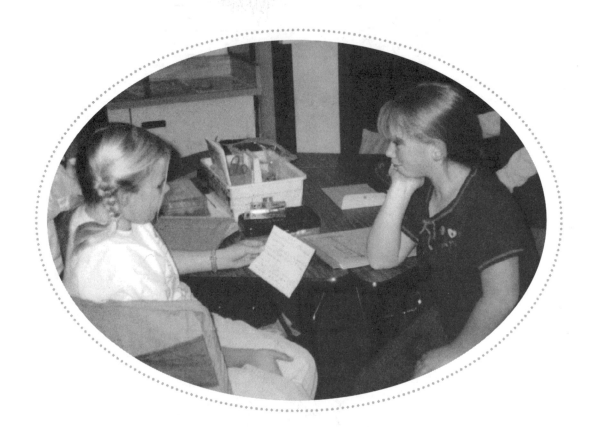

U nderstanding multiplication lays the groundwork for solving more complicated math problems. If we want students to be able to estimate and solve 52 × 27, they must first have an understanding of what the problem means. Activities that promote a conceptual understanding of multiplication include repeated addition, using arrays and number charts, and solving real-life problems.

STAMP BOOKLET

The "Stamp Booklet" activity simulates the process of designing new stamps for the U.S. Post Office. Students can create any design they want, and they choose the size of the stamp and its value. Then they determine how many of the stamps will fit in a booklet and how much the booklet will cost. Students then present their proposed stamp and booklet to the teacher, who recently has been appointed U.S. Postmaster. During this presentation, students explain how multiplication helped them prepare their booklet and how they calculated its final cost. For an added challenge, you can give students the option of creating several stamp designs, each with its own value. Individual sheets would be made up of multiple copies of the same stamp, but several different sheets could make up a booklet.

IN ADVANCE

Before introducing this activity, I bring either books or sheets of stamps to class and ask students to work in small groups to determine how much each would cost. Students then write about how they solved the problem. I've found students use a variety of strategies, including repeated addition and the calculator, to solve the problem. The written part allows students to explain and reflect on their use of multiplication as a group and gives me insight into their understanding of what multiplication means.

When I introduce the "Stamp Booklet" performance assessment, students are excited about the prospect of designing their own stamps. As you'll see on the anchor papers, students incorporate all sorts of ideas into their stamps—sports items, globes, people, geometric designs, to name just a few. From their written work and oral presentation, you will have a good sense of each student's understanding of multiplication.

Stamp Booklet

NCTM STANDARDS	♦ Understand meanings of operations and how they relate to one another. ♦ Compute fluently and make reasonable estimates. ♦ Select and use various types of reasoning and methods or proof.	♦ Organize and consolidate mathematical thinking through communication. ♦ Communicate their mathematical thinking coherently and clearly to peers, teachers, and others.
BENCHMARKS	♦ Understand the effects of multiplying and dividing whole numbers.	♦ Develop fluency in adding, subtracting, multiplying, and dividing whole numbers.

Performance Assessment Task

The U. S. Post Office is asking for a new stamp design that will be sold in booklets. Create a booklet of your new stamps to present to the U.S. Postmaster. Follow these guidelines:

♦ **Include at least one page of uniquely designed stamps.**

♦ **Label each stamp with its price. Your stamps may be worth any amount. Remember to design groups of stamps of the same value that will fit on sheets in your booklet.**

♦ **Create a cover for the booklet.**

♦ **Include a sheet at the end of the book that gives the following information:**

_____ **the total cost of the book**

_____ **a written explanation of how you used multiplication to determine the cost of the book**

♦ **Present your booklet to your teacher, the newly appointed Postmaster of the U.S. Post Office, in your presentation.**

♦ **Show your stamp booklet.**

♦ **Explain how multiplication was used in your booklet.**

♦ **Tell how you figured out the total cost for the booklet.**

Enabling Skills	♦ understanding what multiplication is ♦ understanding how to use groups to solve a multiplication problem ♦ knowing addition or multiplication facts ♦ communicating mathematical thinking

NAME

DATE

RUBRIC SCORING GUIDE: Stamp Booklet

	In Progress	Basic	Proficient	Advanced
	Partially Proficient			
Understanding Grouping	◆ Work does not show any understanding of how to use groups to solve a problem.	◆ Work does not show how groups were used to solve the problem.	◆ Work demonstrates how groups were used to show the number of stamps and how much they cost.	◆ Work clearly demonstrates how groups were used to show the number of stamps and how much the booklet costs.
Computation	◆ Work is not shown. ◆ More than 5 errors noted in multiplication or addition.	◆ Not all work is shown. ◆ Multiplication or addition errors noted.	◆ Work is shown. ◆ Work may have 1-2 multiplication or addition errors.	◆ All work is shown. ◆ Work is correct.
Neatness	◆ Stamp book is extremely messy. ◆ There is no color, or it is difficult to read.	◆ Stamp book looks plain. ◆ It may be a bit messy, have little color, or be difficult to read.	◆ Stamp book is creatively done. ◆ It is neatly done, has color, and can easily be read and understood.	◆ Stamp book is original. ◆ It is very neat, has a lot of color, and looks like a professional completed it.
Oral Presentation	◆ Presentation is very unclear. ◆ There are no connections made between math and the stamp booklet.	◆ Presentation does not clearly explain how multiplication was used. ◆ Student has difficulty explaining the solution. ◆ Postmaster has many questions.	◆ Presentation explains how multiplication was used to make the book. ◆ Student can explain the solution. ◆ Postmaster has some questions.	◆ Presentation clearly explains how multiplication was used to make the book. ◆ Student can clearly explain solution.

STAMP BOOKLET

♦ **Advanced**

Aaron's stamp booklet scored in the Advanced range in all areas. By looking at his written work, you can easily tell that he has ten 20-cent stamps, ten 15-cent stamps, and ten 10-cent stamps. His written work indicates that he used repeated addition to solve the cost of each stamp, and then added those prices together to determine the total cost. His book was creatively and colorfully done, and his presentation to the Postmaster indicates a solid understanding of the concept of multiplication.

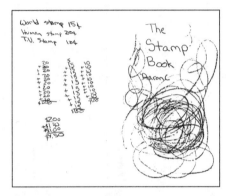

▲ **Advanced Performance Assessment for Stamp Booklet**

♦ **Proficient**

Jake's stamp booklet scored mostly in the Proficient range. As you look at how he determined the cost, he grouped numbers together (i.e., 5 + 5 = 10, 5 + 5 = 10). Although this is a legitimate way to find the total cost, it is not the most effective way of demonstrating how multiplication can be used to solve the problem. His stamp book is neatly done and can be easily read and understood, also scoring in the proficient range for neatness. His verbal presentation is strong and clearly explained how multiplication is used to make the book, thus scoring in the Advanced range.

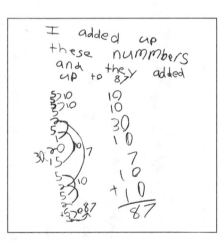

▲ **Proficient Performance Assessment for Stamp Booklet**

♦ **To Share with Students**

When showing these anchor papers to students, I point out the difference between Aaron's and Jake's solutions. I discuss what Jake could have done to improve his work to the Advanced level, namely using a more effective means of computing the cost of the booklet, neater stamps, and a more creative cover. Discussing this with students helps them understand the difference between the two levels.

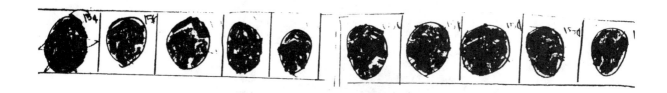

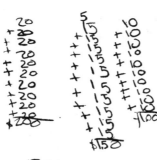

World stamp 15¢
Human stamp 20¢
T.V. Stamp 10¢

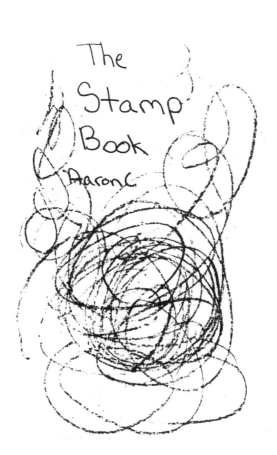

The
Stamp
Book
Aaron C

I added up
these nummbers
and they added
up to 87

5 10   19
5 10   10
5   30
2
5   10
1
30 20 10 7   7
15
5   10
3   10   + 10
5   ———
2   87
+5 87

Jake

Division

Understanding division becomes easier when students see the connection between it and other operations. Consequently, I've found it best to introduce division shortly after students have mastered multiplication. During our study of division, I concentrate on three parts: sharing, grouping, and the remainder.

Division problems fall into one of two categories: sharing or grouping. Dividing 6 cookies among 3 friends is an example of sharing. You know among how many friends want to share the cookies you have—your answer tells you how many cookies each friend will get. In this case, sharing six cookies among three friends means that each friend will get two cookies.

Grouping involves splitting a number of objects into groups of a predetermined size. For instance, if I am giving away 50 stickers and want to give each student five stickers, how many students will receive stickers? In this case, I know the total number of items I have (as in sharing) and the number of items I want in a group; the question is, how many groups can I form? In this case, I could give five stickers to ten students.

QUEEN ANT

To introduce the performance assessment for this unit, I read the students *One Hundred Hungry Ants* by Elinor Pinczes. This delightful story tells of one ant's ideas about the most efficient way to get 100 ants from the colony to a picnic. The book describes five different ways that the colony could be divided in order to get to the picnic. Unfortunately, the picnic is over by the time the ants get there because they spent so much time arranging themselves into the possible groupings!

For the "Queen Ant" assessment, students become queen of their own ant colony and decide how many ants live there. Having students select the number of ants in their colony allows the needs of individual students to be met. I encourage my more capable students to select a greater number of ants. For those students who are still struggling, I encourage them to select a lesser number and use manipulatives to assist them in determining the different groupings. All students must select a number of ten or higher so that they will always be dealing with whole numbers. Then students list how many ants there would be in each group if they traveled in one line, two lines, three lines, all the way to ten lines of ants. Since students are the queen ants, they decide how the colony proceeds to the picnic by issuing a proclamation.

REMAINDER

I've found that the best way to help students understand remainder is to give them lots of practice with problems involving remainders. Using manipulatives, working with other students, and talking as a whole class about the subject all help students discover this important concept.

NAME _____   DATE

Queen Ant

NCTM STANDARDS	◆ Understand meanings of operations and how they relate to one another. ◆ Compute fluently and make reasonable estimates.	◆ Solve problems that arise in mathematics and in other contexts. ◆ Select and use various types of reasoning and methods of proof.
BENCHMARKS	◆ Understand various meanings of multiplication and division. ◆ Understand the effects of multiplying and dividing whole numbers.	◆ Develop fluency in adding, subtracting, multiplying, and dividing whole numbers. Understand the effects of multiplying and dividing whole numbers.

Performance Assessment Task

As queen of the ant colony, it is your job to see that your colony gets to the picnic in the quickest way possible. If you're too slow, you may miss out altogether on any delicious morsels of food! Follow these steps to complete your task:

◆ **Determine how many ants are in your colony.**

◆ **Figure out what would happen if your ants tried to group themselves into one line, two lines, three lines, and so on up to ten lines. How many ants would be in each line?**

◆ **Record your answers like this:**

_____ **Hungry Ants**

one lines of   _____
two line of   _____
three lines of   _____

and so on, until you have completed ten lines.

◆ **Based on your answers, determine which grouping would be the most efficient way to move the ants to the picnic.**

◆ **Make a proclamation that can be displayed at the colony telling the ants what kind of line they should form to go to the picnic. Explain why the ants need to line up in that particular formation.**

Enabling Skills	◆ dividing whole numbers evenly ◆ dividing whole numbers with remainders ◆ spelling correctly

10 Ready-to-Go Math Performance Assessments by Ruth Melendez   Scholastic Professional Books

NAME

DATE

RUBRIC SCORING GUIDE: Queen Ant

	In Progress Partially Proficient	Basic	Proficient	Advanced
Division Work	◆ Student does not understand division. ◆ Many errors in work noted. ◆ Remainder not given. ◆ Student needs a lot of help from the teacher.	◆ Student's understanding of division seems a little shaky. ◆ Three to four errors noted in division work. ◆ Remainder may or may not be given. ◆ Student may need some help from the teacher.	◆ Student seems to understand division. ◆ One to two errors noted in work. ◆ Remainder is given. ◆ Student needs little, if any, help from the teacher.	◆ Division work is perfect. ◆ All answers are correct. ◆ If there is a remainder, it is stated. ◆ No assistance needed from the teacher.
Proclamation	◆ Reason for formation is not given or supported. ◆ The ants wouldn't know what to do.	◆ Reason for formation is given but is not thought out or reasonable. ◆ Reason is not supported by math work. ◆ The ants would be a little confused about how to line up.	◆ Reason given for formation is thought out and fairly reasonable. ◆ Reason may or may not be supported. ◆ The ants would understand what to do.	◆ Reason for formation is well thought out and reasonable. ◆ The reason is supported. ◆ The ants would understand what they need to do and why.
Conventions	◆ Five or more convention errors noted. ◆ Poster is messy and difficult to read.	◆ Three to four convention errors noted on poster. ◆ Poster is not colorful but is readable.	◆ One to two convention errors noted on poster. ◆ Poster may or may not have color. It is easy to read.	◆ Poster doesn't have any convention errors. ◆ Poster is colorful and easy to read.

QUEEN ANT

♦ **Advanced**

Jenni selected 30 ants for her colony, and then correctly put them into ten lines without any assistance from me. Her proclamation gives a reason that is well thought out: The ants would easily understand how they need to line up. Her artwork is colorful, clear, and easy to read. She earned Advanced in all

♦ areas.

30 Hungry Ants

1 line of 30
2 lines of 15
3 lines of 10
4 lines of 7R2
5 lines of 6
6 lines of 5
7 lines of 4R2
8 lines of 3R6
9 lines of 3R3
10 lines of 3

▲ **Advanced Performance Assessment for Queen Ant**

♦ **Proficient**

Natalie's ant colony had 50 hungry ants. She made one error on her division work, thus scoring in the Proficient range. Three lines of 17 with a remainder of 1 does not equal 50. It should have been 3 lines of 16 with a remainder of 2. She also scored in the Proficient range for conventions because she misspelled *because* and because her reason is not expressed in a complete sentence. Her proclamation, however, was well thought out, supported, and the ants would have understood what to do. She scored in the Advanced range in this

♦ area.

50 Hungry Ants

1 line of 50
2 lines of 25
3 lines of 17 R1
4 lines of 12 R2
5 lines of 10
6 lines of 8 R2
7 lines of 7 R1
8 lines of 6 R2
9 lines of 5 R5
10 lines of 5

▲ **Proficient Performance Assessment for Queen Ant**

30 Hungry Ants

1 line of 30

2 lines of 15

3 lines of 10

4 lines of 7R2

5 lines of 6

6 lines of 5

7 lines of 4R2

8 lines of 3R6

9 lines of 3R3

10 lines of 3

I think the ants should go in 10 lines of 3, because it is faster if the lines would be short!!

Jenni

50 Hungry Ants
by Natalie

10 lines of 50.
50 % 10 = 5

Why?

Beacuse the
less (few) ants in each
line the faster
we move!

50 Hungry Ants
1 line of 50
2 lines of 25
3 lines of 17 R1
4 lines of 12 R2
5 lines of 10
6 lines of 8 R2
7 lines of 7 R1
8 lines of 6 R2
9 lines of 5 R5
10 lines of 5

Probability

Probability is a unit that often doesn't get a lot of attention in the mathematics classroom. It goes hand in hand, however, with a study of data and statistics. For instance, students could collect data to answer the following question: *What is the likelihood that the sun will shine in Colorado Springs during the month of September?* Students could answer this question by recording the number of sunny days during the month, and then writing a fraction to represent the number of days out of 30 that the sun actually did shine.

During a study of probability, students should be introduced to mathematical words such as *likely, equally likely, unlikely, certain, uncertain, impossible, chance, fair,* and *unfair.* I've used several activities to introduce and teach these concepts. Spinners, two different colors of tiles or counters, different colored beans, coins, and dice are among the many manipulatives I've found effective when teaching probability concepts and vocabulary.

IS IT FAIR?

"Is It Fair?" asks students to design a game for a commercial game company using a spinner or dice. Students also have to discuss in writing whether and why their game is fair or unfair (see reproducible on page 61). During the revision process, students play one another's games and give feedback about the clarity of directions, neatness, and discussion of fairness. Students have found this feedback quite helpful as they prepare their final product.

IN ADVANCE

It's important that before administering the performance assessment for this unit, you introduce students to the concept of whether a game is fair. Spinner games, dice games, and even the children's game Rock, Paper, Scissors can be used to discuss this concept. All these games give each player an equal chance to win, so they are fair.

Students love this unit. Those who struggle with computation often grasp probability concepts. And all students enjoy using the different manipulatives and playing games. When the unit is finished, you have a wide selection of games to put on your game shelf that students can play throughout the year.

NAME _____   DATE _____

Is It Fair?

NCTM STANDARDS	◆ Understand and apply basic concepts of probability. ◆ Develop and evaluate mathematical arguments and proofs. ◆ Communicate mathematical thinking coherently and clearly to peers,	teachers, and others. ◆ Use the language of mathematics to express mathematical ideas precisely. ◆ Create and use representations to organize, record, and communicate mathematical ideas.
BENCHMARKS	◆ Describe events as likely or unlikely and discuss the degree of likelihood	using words such as *certain, equally likely,* and *impossible*.

Performance Assessment Task

The RAM company, which specializes in super-fun games, is looking for games designed by kids to sell to other kids. Create your own game, and then test it to make sure it's fair. Follow these steps:

♦ **Think of a game you could invent that uses dice, a spinner, tiles, or cards.**

♦ **Fill out the attached game worksheet. Spelling, capital letters, and periods do count! Make sure your rules are clearly explained. Your explanation about why your game is fair or unfair should contain *at least four math words*.**

♦ **Design your game board. Neatness and color are important!**

Enabling Skills	◆ Thinking of a game you want to design ◆ Understanding what makes a game fair or unfair ◆ Using probability words to explain why game is fair or unfair ◆ Checking spelling, capital letters, and periods ◆ Designing a neat, colorful, and creative game board

NAME _____

DATE _____

RUBRIC SCORING GUIDE: Is It Fair?

	In Progress / Partially Proficient	Basic	Proficient	Advanced
Game Board	◆ A kid would not pick this as a game to play. ◆ There's no color, and it's messy.	◆ A kid would play the game if you asked him to. ◆ The board doesn't have much color. ◆ The board doesn't draw players into the game.	◆ A kid would want to play this game. ◆ The board is colorful and neatly done.	◆ A kid would be eager to play this game. ◆ It is colorful, creative, and neatly done. ◆ Has title of game on the board.
Explanation	◆ No math language was used.	◆ At least 2 math words were appropriately used.	◆ At least 3 math words were appropriately used.	◆ At least 4 math words were appropriately used.
Directions	◆ It's not clear how to play this game.	◆ Explanation is fairly clear. ◆ One could begin playing after having two or more questions answered.	◆ Explanation is clear. ◆ One could begin playing after having one question answered.	◆ Detailed explanation of how to play the game. ◆ One could begin playing without any questions.
Conventions	◆ Numerous errors in spelling, capitalization, grammar, or punctuation. ◆ Worksheet is difficult to read.	◆ There are several errors in spelling, capitalization, grammar, or punctuation. Worksheet is readable.	◆ There are a few errors in spelling, capitalization, grammar, and punctuation. Errors don't take away from the worksheet.	◆ There aren't any errors in spelling, capitalization, grammar, or punctuation. ◆ It is easy to read.

IS IT FAIR?

♦ **Advanced**

Aaron's game board is clearly designed and colorfully done. Many students enjoyed playing his game. His directions are detailed and easy to follow. His explanation of whether his game is fair is complete and uses at least four math words, and his overall conventions are strong.

Is It Fair?
A Look at Probability
Invent a Game Worksheet

Name of game Pick a tile
Authors Aaron

Number of players 2-4
Materials needed a brown paper bag and 3 red tiles, 5 blue tiles, and 2 yellow tiles, a gameboard and a different color tile for every player.
Rules for play First you put all of the tiles in a bag. Then you take turns drawing a tile out of the bag. If you draw a tile, you put it back in and shake the bag up. If you draw a red tile, you move 5 spaces, a blue tile and you move 1 space, or a yellow and you move 10 spaces.
This game is ☑ fair ☐ unfair because everyone has the same chance of drawing any tile because you put the tile back in the bag when your'e done drawing it. There is a 50-50 chance of drawing a blue or a yellow, but you don't have an equally likely chance of getting red, because there are less red than blue and yellow.

©1995 CUISENAIRE CO. OF AMERICA, INC., PO Box 5026, White Plains, NY 10602-5026

▲ Advanced Performance Assessment for Is It Fair?

♦ **Proficient**

Alex's work scores in the Proficient range. Although he uses some color, his board wasn't as inviting as Aaron's board. He uses three math words in his explanation, and most students and the teacher had to ask one question prior to beginning to play his game. The most common questions were, "Do I roll one die or two?" and "Do I roll the dice to play the game?" These details are not clearly spelled out in his directions. His spelling, capital letters, and periods are strong; however, he has one grammatical error and he wrote the word *that* twice in a row on his directions, an editing error. This assessment scored entirely in the Proficient range.

Is It Fair?
A Look at Probability
Invent a Game Worksheet

Name of game get to the finish
Authors Alex M.

Number of players 2-4
Materials needed 2 dice, game pieces as in colored tiles, game bord.

Rules for play Roll the dice, who ever gets the highest number goes first. If you land on a spot that the color is green you move ahead 5 spaces. But if you get a two on the dice or land on a place that that is red you lose a turn. If you land on a space that says back go back to start you half to go back to the start. The last thing who ever gets to the finish wins.
This game is ☐ fair ☑ unfair because There is more chances to get lose a turn then there is go ahead spaces so that is just unfair.

▲ Proficient Performance Assessment for Is It Fair?

Is It Fair?
A Look at Probability
Invent a Game Worksheet

Name of game Pick a tile

Authors Aaron

Number of players 2-4

Materials needed a brown paper bag and 3 red tiles, 5 blue tiles, and 2 yellow tiles, a gameboard and a different color tile for every player.

Rules for play

First you put all of the tiles in a bag. Then you take turns drawing a tile out of the bag. If you draw a tile, you put in back in and shake the bag up. If you draw a red tile, you move your tile 5 spaces, a blue tile and you move 1 space, or a yellow and you move 10 spaces.

This game is ☑ fair ☐ unfair because everyone has the same chance of drawing any tile because you put the tile back in the bag when your'e done drawing it. There is a 50-50 chance of drawing a blue or a yellow, but you don't have an equally likely chance of getting red, because there are less red than blue and yellow.

Is It Fair?
A Look at Probability
Invent a Game Worksheet

Name of game get to the finish

Authors Alex M.

Number of players 2-4

Materials needed 2 dice, game pieces as in colored tiles, game bord.

Rules for play Roll the dice, who ever gets the highest number goes first. If you land on a spot that the color isgreenyou move ahead 5 spaces. But if you get a two on the dice or land on a place that that is red you lose a turn. If you land on a space that says back.
go back to start you half to go back to the start. The last thing who ever gets to the finish wins.

This game is ☐ fair ☒ unfair because There is more chances to get lose a turn then there is go ahead spaces so that is just unfair.

Is It Fair?

Name of Game _____

Designed by: _____

Number of Players:_____

Materials Needed: _____

_____

_____

Rules: _____

_____

_____

_____

_____

_____

Is your game fair or unfair? On the lines below tell what type of game you developed
and WHY! Be sure to include math words in your explanation.

_____

_____

_____

_____

_____

_____

_____

Adapted form Cuisenaire Co. of America

Measurement

We all ask ourselves questions such as, *How far is it to my friend's house? How tall am I? How much does my backpack weigh? What is the temperature today? How much will this cup hold?* The answer to each of these questions requires some sort of measurement, whether it be distance, length, weight, temperature, or volume. Intermediate-grade students are ready to tackle these kinds of problems, and a unit on measurement should actively involve them in determining the appropriate unit to measure an object or space, estimating its size, and then performing the actual measurement.

MEASUREMENT OLYMPICS

My unit on measurement culminates with the "Measurement Olympics" performance assessment. I divide the class into small groups of two to three and ask each group to design and write directions for a measurement event that can be done in the classroom. I present examples of past events to whet their appetites and give them ideas. Then I invite the class to brainstorm other possible events. They break into groups and work out the details of their event. I find it helpful to have each group ask for my approval for their event. This ensures no duplication of events and that all events can be done in the space allowed.

My students took two class periods to design and prepare the event and two days to complete the ten different Olympic events. Before groups prepare their final copy of directions, it is helpful to ask another group to read their directions and give them feedback. *Do you understand this event? What questions do you have?* and *What convention errors do you see?* are all questions that provide valuable feedback to students.

To help me assess student performance on this task, I provide each student with a recording sheet (see page 69). Students use this sheet to record their estimates and actual measurements for each event, which lets me see if their estimates were reasonable. In addition, each student indicates on the recording sheet how clear and useful the directions were for each event. Taking anecdotal notes on the dynamics of each group will help you complete the group-work behavior portion of the rubric.

These are a few of the past events I share with my students each year.

JAVELIN THROW

1. Stand on a line and throw a straw as far as possible.
2. Estimate the distance the straw traveled and then measure the distance.
3. Record the estimate and the actual measurement on the recording sheet.

SPONGE SQUEEZE

1. Dip a sponge in water and then squeeze the saturated sponge into container marked with milliliters.
2. Estimate the amount of water squeezed out and then read the measurement from the cup.
3. Record the estimate and measurement on the recording sheet.

MANAGEMENT TIP

I assign each group an event to begin with and rotate them to the next event approximately every ten minutes. I post a map of the events and the rotation schedule at various places around the room.

NAME _____   DATE _____

Measurement Olympics

NCTM STANDARDS	♦ Understand measurable attributes of objects and the units, systems, and processes of measurement. ♦ Apply appropriate techniques, tools, and formulas to determine measurements. ♦ Use the language of mathematics to	express mathematical ideas precisely. ♦ Recognize and apply mathematics in contexts outside of mathematics. ♦ Create and use representations to organize, record, and communicate mathematical ideas.
BENCHMARKS	♦ Understand the need for measuring with standard units and become familiar with standard units in the customary and metric systems.	♦ Select and apply appropriate standard units and tools to measure length. ♦ Select and use benchmarks to estimate measurements.

Performance Assessment Task

You and your group have been asked to design an event for the Measurement Olympics. Each event will require the use of some type of measurement. Here's a specific breakdown of your task:

♦ **Design a measuring task that can be completed safely in the classroom.**

♦ **As a group, write directions for the event. Prepare a final copy. Capital letters, periods, and spelling do count!**

♦ **On Olympic day, set up your event.**

♦ **You and your group will go from event to event, reading the directions, completing the events, and marking your measurements on your recording sheet. First, you will estimate your performance at the event and record it on the sheet. After you have tried the event, you need to measure your performance and write an exact measurement. Some measurements will need to be written as a fraction. Then, figure the difference between your estimate and your exact measurement. Finally, evaluate the activity directions. Were they clear, just so-so, or not clear at all?**

♦ **Your group will be responsible for tearing down your event.**

Enabling Skills	♦ identifying labeling units correctly ♦ writing fractions correctly ♦ writing clear, concise directions ♦ writing with correct spelling, capital letters, and periods ♦ working together as a group

10 Ready-to-Go Math Performance Assessments by Ruth Melendez Scholastic Professional Books

NAME _____

DATE _____

RUBRIC SCORING GUIDE: Measurement Olympics

	Partially Proficient		**Proficient**	**Advanced**
	In Progress	**Basic**		
Directions	◆ Directions are unclear and unorganized. ◆ Contestants wouldn't know what to do. ◆ Convention errors are so numerous that it is difficult to read.	◆ Directions are a little confusing. ◆ Contestants would have several questions about what to do. ◆ There are fewer than 6 convention errors.	◆ Directions for the event are satisfactory. ◆ Contestants might have one question about what to do. ◆ There are fewer than 4 convention errors.	◆ Directions for the event are well written and easy to understand. ◆ Contestants could complete the event without any help. ◆ One would have to look for convention errors.
Estimates	◆ Student does not attempt to make logical estimates.	◆ Estimates are poor. Logical thinking isn't apparent.	◆ Estimates are made with some logical thinking apparent.	◆ Logical thinking is apparent in student's estimates.
Measurements	◆ Measurements are not written correctly or aren't labeled. ◆ Many errors noted in writing fractions.	◆ Several measurements are written incorrectly or are not labeled. ◆ Several errors noted in writing fractions.	◆ Most measurements are written correctly and labeled. ◆ Most fractions are written correctly.	◆ Measurements have the appropriate units and are written correctly. ◆ Fractions, if needed, are written correctly.
Group Work	◆ Students cannot complete task because of so many conflicts.	◆ Teacher must intervene in several conflicts.	◆ Students had a few conflicts that the teacher needed to mediate.	◆ Students worked together well. They solved conflicts by themselves.

MEASUREMENT OLYMPICS

◆ Advanced

The directions for the Advanced sample completed by Group 1 are easy to understand. Contestants completed the event without any assistance and indicated on their recording sheets that the directions were well written. There are no spelling errors.

The recording sheet on page 68 falls within the Advanced range. All measurements are clearly labeled and the estimates are reasonable. The calculations are correct, and all directions were evaluated.

Javelin Throw

1. Put your toe behind the masking tape line.

2. Take the straw and throw it as far as you can.

3. Estimate in centimeters how far you threw it. Put your estimate on your recording sheet.

4. Measure using the measuring tape how far you really did throw it. Put your exact answer on your recording sheet.

5. Before you leave, return the straw and measuring tape to the masking tape line.

6. On your recording sheet, tell what you think about our directions. Yes, no or so-so?

BY: GROUP 1

▲ **Advanced Performance Assessment for Measurement Olympics**

◆ Proficient

The directions for the Proficient sample, completed by Group 3 are satisfactory; however, many of the contestants indicated that the directions are just so-so. Some questions contestants asked include: *What unit of measurement am I using to measure the water? Do I just leave the water in the container? Or should I dump it back into the tub where the sponge is?* There are three convention errors. Direction number three mistakenly has the word *your* instead of *you*. Number four has a period instead of a question mark, and the word *really* is misspelled.

Sponge Squeeze

1. Dip the sponge in the water.

2. Squeeze the water into the container.

3. How much water do you think your squeezed out? Write this on your recording sheet.

4. Look at the container. How much water did you realy squeeze out. Write this on your recording sheet.

5. Put the sponges back in the water when you leave.

BY: GROUP 3

▲ **Proficient Performance Assessment for Measurement Olympics**

◆ Assessment Note

This assessment evaluates both group work and the individual student's recording sheet. Each member of the group receives the same rating for the directions and the group work, but receives the individual ratings for their estimates and measurements.

Javelin Throw

1. Put your toe behind the masking tape line.

2. Take the straw and throw it as far as you can.

3. Estimate in centimeters how far you threw it. Put your estimate on your recording sheet.

4. Measure using the measuring tape how far you really did throw it. Put your exact answer on your recording sheet.

5. Before you leave, return the straw and measuring tape to the masking tape line.

6. On your recording sheet, tell what you think about our directions. Yes, no or so-so?

BY: GROUP 1

Sponge Squeeze

1. Dip the sponge in the water.

2. Squeeze the water into the container.

3. How much water do you think your squeezed out? Write this on your recording sheet.

4. Look at the container. How much water did you realy squeeze out. Write this on your recording sheet.

5. Put the sponges back in the water when you leave.

BY: GROUP 3

Olympics Recording Sheet

Chris _____ Name

Name of Event	Estimate	Exact Measurement	Difference	Directions Clear? Yes, So-So, No
School Walk	100 steps	152 steps	48 steps	so-so
Toss up	55 1/4 inches	62 3/4 inches	7 1/4 inches	no
Cotton ball shot put	3 yards	2 1/4 yards	3/4 yards	yes
footsteps	30 steps	31 steps	1 step	so-so
Flicking Paper	7 ft.	6 1/2 ft.	1/2 ft.	yes
Relay team	30 sec.	36 sec.	6 sec.	no
Javelin Throw	1 ft	2 ft	1 ft	yes
Standing Long jump	4 ft	3 ft	1 ft	yes
Spoon Toss	5.5 ft	7 ft	1.5 ft	yes
Sponge Squeeze	25 ml	30 ml	5 ml	so-so

Olympics Recording Sheet

Name _____

Name of Event	Estimate	Exact Measurement	Difference	Directions Clear? Yes, So-So-, No

Area

A lthough students may have explored the concept of area, the formal introduction of this topic usually occurs in third grade. Here, students learn to use standard units and tools for measuring, develop the ability to estimate the area, and use formulas to determine area. Typically, I cover area after multiplication because it gives students the opportunity to apply their knowledge of multiplication.

I use the following activity to help students discover the standard formula for determining area. First, I cut out several rectangles of varying size from a transparency and label each (A, B, C, etc.). Then I make a transparency of centimeter grid paper and place it on the overhead. I select one of the rectangles and put it on top of the transparency. I ask students to determine the length and width of the rectangle by counting the centimeter squares along each edge of the rectangle. Next, I ask them to count the total number of squares the rectangle covers. Students record this information on their copy of the grid shown at right. (I distribute a blank copy to each student at the beginning of this activity.) We repeat this process for another rectangle, and then pause to discuss what we see. I ask students if they notice any relationship between the length, width, and area. If they do, I ask them how they would describe the relationship. We continue studying the rest of the rectangles to confirm what we notice; ultimately students discover the formula: length × width = area.

Rectangle	Length (cm)	Width (cm)	Area (cm2)
A	5	4	20
B	4	4	16
C	1	5	5
D	2	6	
E	4	3	

Activity taken from NCTM Principles and Standards for Mathematics, 2000.

YOU BE THE JUDGE

The performance assessment for my unit on area asks students to serve as judges in Kids' Court. Their first case requires them to use their knowledge of area to make a fair decision: Four friends agreed to a painting project at a local miniature golf course for $12.00. They completed the job but then disagreed about how to split the fee. Each friend painted one wall, but each wall was a different shape. My students, as judges, must determine how to fairly distribute the money among the four painters. I charge my students to make a fair decision and to explain their thinking

TIP

I use centimeter paper for this activity and give the dimensions of the walls in centimeters. This makes it easier for students to draw the walls and compute the areas.

NAME _____   DATE _____

You Be the Judge

NCTM STANDARDS	◆ Understand measurable attributes of objects and the units, systems, and processes of measurement.	arguments and proofs.
	◆ Solve problems that arise in mathematics and in other contexts.	◆ Organize and consolidate mathematical thinking through communication.
	◆ Develop and evaluate mathematical	◆ Recognize and apply mathematics in contexts outside of mathematics.
BENCHMARKS	◆ Understand attributes such as length and area, and select the	appropriate type of unit for measuring each attribute.

Performance Assessment Task

Today is your first day as the Honorable Judge of the Kids' Court. This is a very important position because you will be making decisions that affect kids. Here is your first case:

Four kids were hired to complete a painting project at a local miniature golf course. The kids' contract says that they would be paid a total of $12.00. When the kids were paid, they couldn't decide how to share the money because the wall each kid painted wasn't the same shape. Your job as judge is to determine whether the kids painted the same area and whether they should each receive the same amount of money.

To make a fair decision, you need to conduct the following investigation:

◆ Draw a diagram on centimeter grid paper of each wall that was painted on paper.

◆ Determine the area of each wall.

◆ Write your decision giving your opinion of how the money should be divided. Your decision should contain math words to explain your thinking.

Dimension of walls   10 X 4 cm   8 X 5 cm   9 X 3 cm   8 X 4 cm

Enabling Skills	◆ understanding area
	◆ calculating area
	◆ recalling addition and multiplication facts

10 Ready-to-Go Math Performance Assessments by Ruth Melendez Scholastic Professional Books

NAME

DATE

RUBRIC SCORING GUIDE: You Be the Judge

| | In Progress | Basic | Proficient | Advanced |
	Partially Proficient			
Math Work	• Student appears not to understand how to figure area.	• The formula for figuring area is correct. • Calculations are wrong. • Arrays are not drawn. • No labels are given.	• Area was figured correctly. • Arrays and answers are shown. • Some answers may not be labeled.	• Area of each shape is correct. • Arrays and answers are shown. • Answers are labeled.
Math Language	• The decision contains no mathematical words.	• The decision contains at least two mathematical words.	• At least 3 mathematical words were used in the decision.	• At least 5 mathematical words were used in the decision.
Court Decision	• The judge's decision was not given or explained. • People do not understand who gets paid what amount.	• Decision was given but not clearly explained. • The total for the four kids does not equal $12.00.	• Decision was explained. • Total for the 4 kids equals $12.00, although it's not clear why.	• Decision was well thought out and clearly explained. • Everyone understands how much each kid should receive.
Conventions	• More than 9 errors in spelling, capital letters, and punctuation. • Decision is messy and difficult to read.	• There are more than 5 errors in spelling, capital letters, or punctuation. • Decision is messy, but still readable.	• There are fewer than 4 errors in spelling, capital letters, or punctuation. • Some messiness doesn't take away from the decision.	• One would have to look carefully for errors in spelling, capital letters, or punctuation. • Court decision is neatly done.

YOU BE THE JUDGE

◆ Advanced

Abigail's assessment falls within the Advanced range in all areas. Her arrays are drawn correctly, the area of each shape is correct and is labeled. Her court decision contains at least five math words, is well thought out, and demonstrates a clear understanding of how much each person would receive. Her writing conventions are excellent.

When sharing this example with students, I make a copy on an overhead transparency and place sticky notes over the answers. Students see a strong example of a court decision, but not the answers!

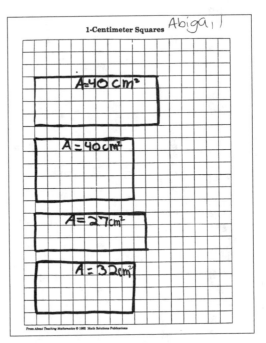

▲ Advanced Performance Assessment for You Be the Judge

◆ Proficient

Corey's math work, court decision, and conventions all fall within the Proficient range. Although he correctly figured the area, he failed to label his answers. He explained why James and Oramis should receive $4.00, but failed to explain the amount Bowser and Yoshi should receive. Corey had one spelling error and left out one punctuation mark and one capital letter. He also left out the word *get* in the second-to-last sentence.

In his explanation, Corey used five math words and scored within the Advanced range for math language.

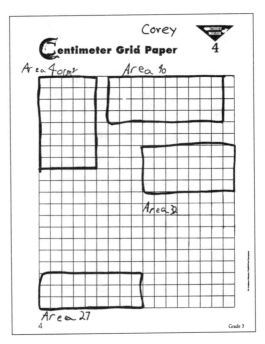

▲ Proficient Performance Assessment for You Be the Judge

1-Centimeter Squares   Abigail

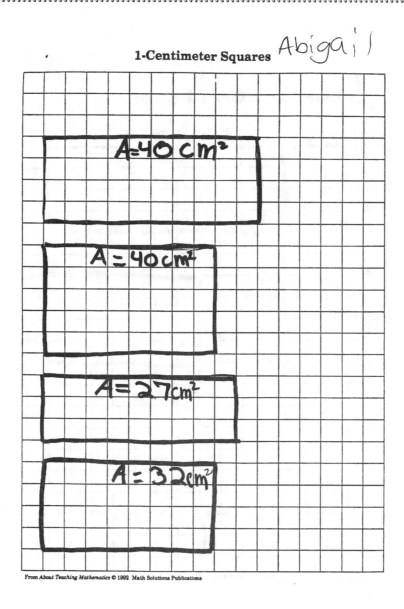

A=40 cm²

A = 40 cm²

A = 27 cm²

A = 32 cm²

From *About Teaching Mathematics* © 1992 Math Solutions Publications

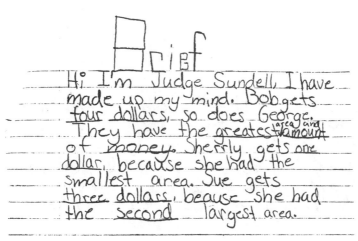

Brief
Hi I'm Judge Sundell, I have
made up my mind. Bob gets
four dollars, so does George.
They have the greatest amount
of money. Sherrly gets one
dollar, because she had the
smallest area. Sue gets
three dollars, beause she had
the second largest area.

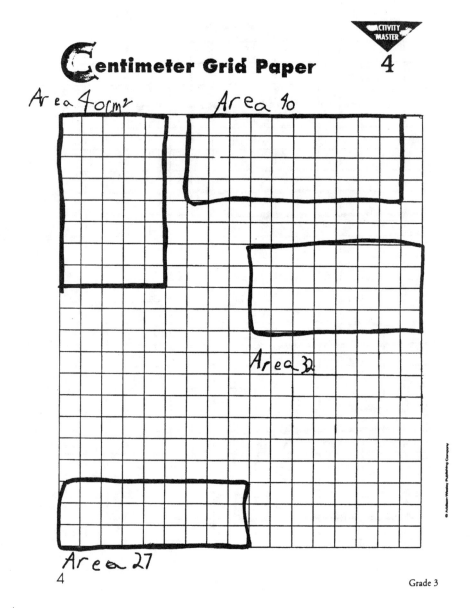

ACTIVITY MASTER

Centimeter Grid Paper

4

Area 40cm²   Area 40

Area 32

Area 27

4

Grade 3

I think that James and Oramer should get ~~four dollars~~ because they did the same size and the biggest! Bowser should get three dollars and Koshi should get one dollar. That's what I think.

Corey

Tessellations

A *tessellation* is an infinite set of shapes that covers an entire plane without overlapping or leaving any gaps. During the study of tessellations, I encourage students to look for the geometric patterns in our everyday lives. This unit confirms the notion that mathematics is much more than computation, and it gives students the opportunity to sort, build, draw, model, trace, and construct different shapes. During this process, students are constructing knowledge about geometric concepts, such as sliding, flipping, and turning. Dot paper, graphing paper, and plain paper are used to create different types of tessellations.

During a tessellation unit, students usually explore the following questions: *Which shapes tessellate? Why will certain shapes tessellate and others not? How many different tessellating patterns can we create using two or more regular polygons? Do tessellating designs have symmetry? How can we use slides, flips, and turns to create unique tessellations?* After students have developed their understanding of tessellations, they create their own unique design for the performance assessment.

A-MAZE-ING TESSELLATIONS

For this assessment, I invented the Maze Art Company. The company recently decided to incorporate tessellation designs on several of their products and are soliciting tessellation designs from students. The request is for a tessellation that uses at least two different colors. Students create their own design and then write a letter to accompany their tessellation describing the shapes they used, where they got their idea, and why their design should be selected. Their letter must contain some math words to describe their thinking.

This unit is a favorite among students. I like to use it at the beginning of the year to get students excited about math and to reinforce the notion that math is much more than paper and pencil tasks. Some teachers I know use it at the end of the year so that students finish the term with positive feelings about math. Whenever you choose to use it, you'll find the students excited and engaged.

NAME

DATE

A-Maze-ing Tessellations

NCTM STANDARD(S)	♦ Analyze characteristics and properties of two-dimensional geometric shapes and develop mathematical arguments about geometric	relationships. ♦ Apply transformations and use symmetry to analyze mathematical situations.
BENCHMARKS	♦ Investigate, describe, and reason about the results of subdividing, combining, and transforming shapes.	♦ Predict and describe the results of sliding, flipping, and turning two-dimensional shapes.

Performance Assessment Task

The Maze Art Company is adding tessellation designs to several new products. The company is encouraging people to submit original tessellations. The best ones will be purchased by the company.

Your task has three parts to it:

♦ **Make a tessellation using any type of paper you'd like (dot paper, graph paper, plain paper).**

♦ **Color it neatly using at least two different colors.**

♦ **Write a letter to the company describing your design. It MUST include the following:**

   ♦ **shape or shapes you used**

   ♦ **where you got your idea**

   ♦ **why you think your design should be selected as one the company would sell**

   ♦ **several math words to describe your thinking**

Enabling Skills	♦ understanding shapes
	♦ defining tessellation
	♦ making a tessellation
	♦ writing letters

10 Ready-to-Go Math Performance Assessments by Ruth Melendez   Scholastic Professional Books

RUBRIC SCORING GUIDE: A-Maze-ing Tessellations

	Partially Proficient			
	In Progress	Basic	Proficient	Advanced
Tessellations	◆ Student could not make the tessellation without a lot of teacher help.	◆ Student created a design that tessellates. ◆ The student had difficulty covering the surface without any holes or overlapping shapes.	◆ Student created a design that tessellates. ◆ Tessellation covers the surface completely without any holes or overlapping shapes.	◆ Student created his or her own shapes or used at least 2 shapes that tessellate. ◆ It covers the surface completely without any holes or overlapping.
Letter	◆ Both the reason to buy and the source of the idea are missing. ◆ Maze Art Co. won't consider your piece.	◆ The reason to buy or the source of the idea may be missing. ◆ Maze Art Co. doesn't have a strong sense of why your piece should be selected.	◆ A reason to buy and the source of the idea are clearly stated. ◆ Maze Art Co. has some sense of why your piece should be selected.	◆ Reasons to buy and the source of the idea are clearly stated. ◆ Maze Art Co. has a clear sense of why your piece should be selected.
Math Words	◆ No attempt was made to use mathematical terms.	◆ At least 2 mathematical words were used in the letter. ◆ This person may have some difficulty using correct mathematical terms.	◆ At least 3 mathematical words were used in the letter. ◆ This person seems comfortable with math terms.	◆ At least 4 mathematical words were used in the letter. ◆ This person is a whiz at using proper mathematical terms.
Conventions	◆ Letter format is not followed. ◆ Numerous errors in spelling, capital letters, or punctuation make it difficult to read.	◆ Letter format isn't followed. ◆ Several errors in spelling, capital letters, and punctuation are noted, but the letter is readable.	◆ Letter format is followed. ◆ There are a few errors in spelling, capital letters, and punctuation; however, they don't take away from the letter.	◆ Letter format is followed. ◆ There aren't any errors in spelling, capital letters, and punctuation. ◆ It's a pleasure to read.

80

A-MAZE-ING TESSELLATIONS

♦ **Advanced**

Jordan's tessellation falls within the Advanced range in all areas. He created his own shape and used an equilateral triangle to cover the surface completely. He explained in detail where he got his idea and why his tessellation should be purchased. He used the following math words in his letter: *tessellation, equilateral triangle, triangles, square, side,* and *triangle dot paper.* His letter followed the correct format and his conventions are strong.

♦ **Proficient**

Jill's tessellation falls within the Proficient category. She created a design that tessellates, but she used only one shape. Her letter includes a reason to buy her tessellation and where her idea came from; however, her letter is not as strong as Jordan's. She included the following math words: *tessellation, triangle,* and *flipped.* There are a few errors in spelling; however, they don't take away from the letter.

♦ **To Share with the Class**

When sharing these anchor papers with students, I discuss the difference between the two tessellations. Jordan designed his own shape and used two shapes, while Jill used only one shape. Jordan's letter is detailed and strong in math language. Pointing out these specific details helps students see the difference between an Advanced assessment and a Proficient one.

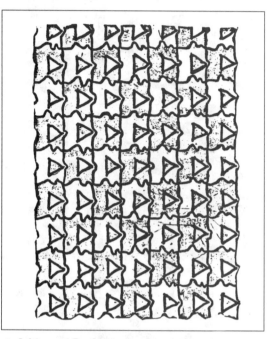

▲ **Advanced Performance Assessment for A-Maze-ing Tessellations**

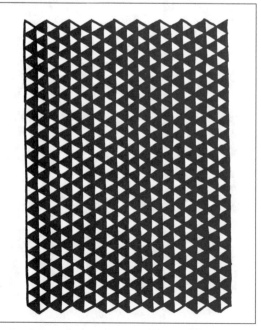

▲ **Proficient Performance Assessment for A-Maze-ing Tessellations**

Jordan

9/15/97

Dear Maze Art Co,

In my tessellation I used a equilateral triangle and my very own shape I made up. I used 63 triangls and 63 shapes that I made.

I got my idea from just snipping around on a little square paper. When I cut one side off I just moved it over to the opposite side. I traced it on triangle dot paper, put the triangle in the middle. I liked so I kept it.

I think my tessellation would look great on a t-shirt or postcard. Think of it. A little girl gets a postcord from Mommy and she says" oh neat postcord." I would just say this tessellation is a good one.

Sincerely,

Jordan

9-22-97

Dear A-Maze-ing Tessellations,
  I have a tessellation for you. I
took a triangle and fliped it so it
covered the page. I got my idea
from a projekt our class did. I
thinck you should buy it because
it looks like a qwilt.
  I hope you have fun.

From,

Jill

CHAPTER 10

Data and Graphing

Data and graphs are everywhere. We see them in newspapers, magazines, on television, and we discuss the information they convey in daily conversations. The recent U.S. census completed by the federal government highlights the importance of data and statistics in our everyday life; the mass of data collected is used to determine congressional districts and what amount of federal dollars will go to which communities. Students need specific skills to understand how to deal with our data-intensive world. They also need skills to evaluate data themselves so that they won't be misled by slick interpretations.

NUMERICAL AND CATEGORICAL DATA

Important during a study of data collection is the students' understanding of different types of data. To highlight the difference between categorical and numerical data, survey your class about the kinds of pets they have. Tally how many cats, dogs, fish, gerbils, and other creatures your students have as pets. This is an example of *categorical data*. Next, ask students how many pets they have; their answer will be the total number of pets in their home. This is an example of *numerical data*. You can remind students of this mini-survey when they are confused about what kind of data they are collecting. Determining what type of data one has as well as how to best represent that data is an important part of learning how to collect and use information.

DATA AND GRAPHING

After collecting and using several types of data, students are ready to tackle a larger project: They can develop their own question, survey a selected population, and record and analyze their results. Two different assessments are included in this chapter. "Lunch Time" explores the all-important question: What is your favorite cafeteria food? Students then make recommendations to the cafeteria manager based on their results. "Party Time" allows students to find out what classmates want to do for a class party and report those results to the party planner.

The rubrics included in the section assess graphing, visual presentation of data, the group oral presentation, and the individual written report. Choose the rubric(s) that suits your particular needs. Examples of proficient and advanced work in each area are included at the back of this chapter.

TIP

Take quick, daily surveys to familiarize students with collecting, representing, and evaluating data. Ask questions such as, *How many brothers and sisters do you have? What is your favorite ice cream?* and *How many pets do you have?*

NAME _____ DATE _____

Party Time!

NCTM STANDARDS	♦ Formulate questions that can be addressed with data and collect, organize, and display relevant data to answer them. ♦ Organize and consolidate mathematical thinking through communication.	♦ Communicate mathematical thinking coherently and clearly to peers, teachers, and others. ♦ Create and use representations to organize, record, and communicate mathematical ideas.
BENCHMARKS	♦ Design investigations to address a question and consider how data collection methods affect the nature of the data set.	♦ Collect data using observations, surveys, and experiments. ♦ Represent data using tables and graphs such as bar graphs and line graphs.

Performance Assessment Task

Our party planner needs help figuring out what to do for our next classroom party. She wants to know what students are most interested in doing. Your group's task is:

♦ **Develop a survey that polls kids about what they want to do for the party.**

♦ **Conduct the survey among your classmates.**

♦ **Construct a professional poster (graph) describing the results of your survey. It can be a bar graph, a pie graph, or a pictograph.**

♦ **Report your findings and make recommendations to your party planner and your math class.**

Enabling Skills	♦ writing a survey
	♦ making a graph (bar, pie, pictograph)
	♦ making posters—colorful, neat, no stray marks, spaced well, catch the reader's attention
	♦ analyzing and reporting your findings
	♦ working together in a group

10 Ready-to-Go Math Performance Assessments by Ruth Melendez Scholastic Professional Books

NAME _____   DATE _____

Lunch Time

NCTM STANDARDS	◆ Formulate questions that can be addressed with data and collect, organize, and display relevant data to answer them. ◆ Organize and consolidate mathematical thinking through communication.	◆ Communicate mathematical thinking coherently and clearly to peers, teachers, and others. ◆ Create and use representations to organize, record, and communicate mathematical ideas.
BENCHMARKS	◆ Design investigations to address a question and consider how data collection methods affect the nature of the data set.	◆ Collect data using observations, surveys, and experiments. ◆ Represent data using tables and graphs such as bar graphs and line graphs.

Performance Assessment Task

The lunchroom staff wants to improve lunch sales at your school. They want to know what your class's lunch preferences are. Your group's task is to:

◆ **Develop a survey about students' favorite vegetable, dessert, or entrée.**

◆ **Conduct the survey in your class.**

◆ **Construct a professional poster (graph) describing the results of your survey. It can be a bar graph, a pie graph, or a pictograph.**

◆ **Report your findings and make recommendations to an employee of the lunchroom.**

◆ **Prepare a group presentation to the cafeteria manager and your class concerning your results.**

Enabling Skills	◆ writing a survey
	◆ making a graph (bar, pie, pictograph)
	◆ making posters that are colorful, neat, with no stray marks, spaced well, and that catch the reader's attention
	◆ working together in a group

NAME

DATE

RUBRIC SCORING GUIDE:
Data and Graphing—Presentation

	In Progress	Basic	Proficient	Advanced
	Partially Proficient			
Group Presentation	◆ Presentation not ready.	◆ Some members participate.	◆ All members participate, but not equally.	◆ All members participate equally.
Data Collection Explanation	◆ Data collection not explained.	◆ Data collection process needs more explanation for understanding.	◆ Data collection process explained adequately.	◆ Data collection process is explained clearly and with confidence.
Explanation of Graph	◆ Graph not explained.	◆ Tells what graph means and makes recommendations with a lot of help from teacher or friends.	◆ Tells what graph means and makes recommendations with a little help from teacher or friends.	◆ Gives a clear report with no help. Tells what graphs means and gives clear recommendations.
Use of Graph in Presentation	◆ Graph not used.	◆ Doesn't point to graph.	◆ Points to graph after being reminded.	◆ Points to graph without being reminded.

NAME

DATE

RUBRIC SCORING GUIDE:
Data and Graphing—Poster

	In Progress Partially Proficient	Basic	Proficient	Advanced
Graph and Poster	◆ Poster not complete.	◆ Poster needs some explanation in order to understand it.	◆ There might be one question about the poster.	◆ Poster needs no explanation. One could understand it just by looking at it.
Poster Labels	◆ Poster not labelled.	◆ Title or labels are missing from poster.	◆ Poster has appropriate title and labels.	◆ Poster has a creative title and creative labels.
Accuracy of Graph	◆ Graph not complete.	◆ Data collected does not match the graph two or more times.	◆ Data collected does not match the graph one time.	◆ Data collected and graph match perfectly!
Neatness	◆ Poster not complete.	◆ Poster is messy. No tools were used, it's hard to read, it's very crowded and has little use of color.	◆ Poster is satisfactory. Some letters may be crooked; it is readable; poster was planned, and has some color.	◆ Poster is great! Letters are straight, it's easy to read, well planned, and is so colorful it grabs your attention.

NAME

DATE

RUBRIC SCORING GUIDE:
Data and Graphing—Report

	In Progress / Partially Proficient	Basic	Proficient	Advanced
Individual Report	◆ Report not finished.	◆ Report includes two true statements about the graph.	◆ Report includes three true statements about the graph.	◆ Report includes five true statements about the graph.
Opinion Statements	◆ Report not finished.	◆ One opinion statement about this activity is given.	◆ Two opinion statements about this activity are given.	◆ Three opinion statements about this activity are given.
Conventions	◆ Report not finished.	◆ Four or more words are misspelled, and 3 or more capital letters and periods are missing.	◆ Two to three words are misspelled. One or two capital letters and periods are missing.	◆ Spelling, capital letters, and periods are perfect!
Neatness	◆ Report not finished.	◆ Report is difficult to read because it is messy.	◆ Report is readable but it takes some effort.	◆ Report looks like a published work of art— very easy to read.

COMMENTS ON DATA ANALYSIS SAMPLES

The photos at right show the results of our class survey regarding favorite class party activities. The group provided four choices from which students could choose. This method prompted a discussion of survey design and how it can affect results. Several students said they would have written in a different activity had they not been limited to the four choices on the survey. The group said that method would have made their job of tallying and representing the data more difficult. Besides, they noted, the write-in choices might not have been practical ideas for a class party. All in all, it was a provocative discussion that helped all students think critically about survey design and results.

These assessments use both the poster/graph rubric as well as the group presentation. According to the poster/graph rubric, the students scored in the Advanced and Proficient range. The graph was easy to understand. It was self-explanatory, well planned, and colorful. The poster has an appropriate title and labels, but doesn't seem to have "creative title or labels." Therefore, I scored this in the Proficient range. An example of a creative title or labels might be a graph that contained some well-designed graphics to go along with

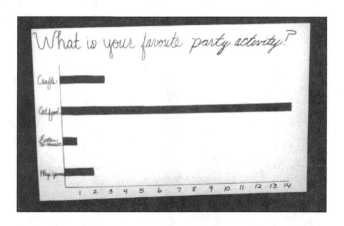

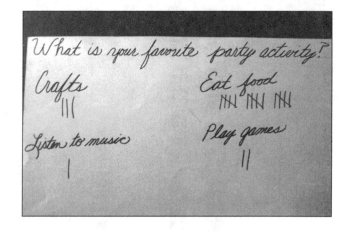

the title or the labels. Looking carefully at the responses, you'll notice that there were 15 responses to "eating food" on the tally sheet, but the graph only shows 14. Therefore, the graph was scored in the Proficient range for this category since there was "one time when the data doesn't match the graph."

COMMENTS ON DATA ANALYSIS SAMPLES

◆ **Advanced**

The examples at right show the graph and tally marks for the question, *What is your favorite lunch dessert?* This assessment scored in the Advanced range in three categories on the graph/poster rubric. The poster needed no explanation, the data collected on the tally sheet matched the graph, and the graph was easy to read, well planned, and colorful. Again, this poster didn't seem to have a "creative title or labels," so I rated that component in the Proficient range.

In following years, I made sure that we discussed the meaning of "creative titles and labels." I also continued to have students role play what Advanced and Proficient group presentation behavior looked like (see below).

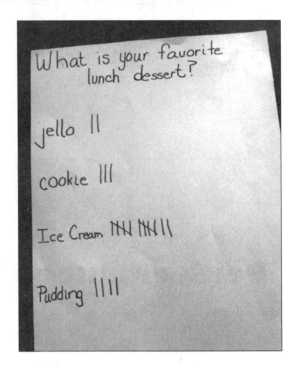

◆ **Role Playing**

Since I can't provide anchor papers for group presentations, I spend time role-playing Advanced and Proficient presentations in class prior to the official presentations. I ask a group of students to role play a presentation in which all members participate equally, and then ask the class to identify the descriptor (Advanced or Proficient). We do this for all four of the indicators: participation, explaining how the data was collected, giving a clear report, and pointing at the graph during the presentation to help clarify their explanation.

NAME _____

DATE _____

NCTM STANDARD(S)

_____

BENCHMARKS

Performance Assessment Task

Enabling Skills

NAME _____

DATE _____

RUBRIC SCORING GUIDE:

Advanced	Proficient	Partially Proficient Basic	In Progress

This book represents my journey toward a more dynamic mathematics classroom. During this journey I discovered many things about my students and myself. Most striking was that performance assessments and rubrics portray a more complete picture of a student's abilities than standard assessments. I learned to delve deeply into my students' writing to understand their thinking, rather than relying purely on a multiple choice test. The students' writing provided more insight into their understanding than a multiple choice test ever could.

This journey helped my students (and me) find the connection between real-life situations and math. Suddenly our lives were full of situations that could be solved using our mathematical knowledge. The concepts that we were studying during class could actually be applied to our daily lives. For the first time, students saw some purpose in what they were learning.

This journey also represents what students can do when given a target and the necessary tools to hit the bullseye. Communicating up front with students through the use of anchor papers displays the target. Providing students with the skills to solve problems and communicate their thinking in writing equips them with necessary tools. When that bullseye is seen by all, students perform beyond my highest expectations. I have learned that thinking does improve and deepen as students continue to communicate their ideas. And as this happens, I see students' confidence in their problem-solving abilities increase. They know they can utilize their understanding of math to solve a problem.

Finally, this journey represents one teacher's dream of having the opportunity to communicate her ideas about mathematics assessment. My hope is that students in your mathematics classroom will benefit from the journey that my students and I took.